DEAR TALIA!

MAY YOUR LIFE BE FILLED WITH

MW01140156

Emma Uche

Adanna cannot wait for her very first day of second grade at a brand new school.

"We've arrived!" shouts her mom from the front seat.

Adanna springs up in her seat and stretches her neck out as far as she can to get a better view of her brand new school.

It looks huge!

"It's time to get out sweetheart. Don't forget your promise." her mom reminds her.

Adanna takes a deep breath before reciting her VOW.

CLICK

"I will be the BEST that I can be Mama!" she proudly exclaims.

"That's my girl!" her mom replies. "Now go on! You don't want to be late on your very first day."

With the sharp CLICK of her seatbelt and in the blink of an eye, Adanna leaps into action and hits the ground running towards the school entrance. She can't wait to see her new classroom.

When Adanna opens the doors she is greeted by a tall woman with long black braids, brown almond-shaped eyes and a wide smile.

"Why, hello there! You must be Adanna." the woman suggests.

"Yes, but how did you know?" Adanna asks

"Because you're the last one left on my list to check in! Good thing you made it here, you're right on time. Welcome to second grade Adanna! I will be your teacher. My name is Miss Erinma!"

Adanna looks up at Miss Erinma. She seems warm and inviting but Adanna is nervous. She had never been to this school before and is not sure what to expect.

"Come on in! Today we will be learning about outer space!" Miss Erinma says.

She offers her hand to Adanna. Adanna grasps it and the two of them go walking down a long hallway filled with bright pictures and paintings on the walls.

When they reach the end of the hall Adanna can hear the voices of the other children and she begins to feel nervous again.

"I will be the best that I can be," she whispers to herself.

When Adanna enters the room, the other children all look at her. They have already been seated and given name tags.

Medina. Elijah. Kelechi. Edward. Kierra. Adanna reads the names silently to herself in her head. The names of her classmates' are interesting, but she knows her own is the best.

"We have one more pupil! Class, say hello to Adanna!" Miss Erinma says

"HELLOOOOOO Adanna!" The class echoes.
"HELLOOOOOO class!" Adanna mimics, with a giggle at the end.

"Okay now, Adanna have a seat! We are about to begin the lesson"

Adanna takes her seat next to Kierra. Kierra's big bright eyes and warm smile welcomed Adanna's presence.

ADANNA

"Okay class, today we will be learning about Outer Space! Who here has heard of outer space?"

"I have!" shouts Kierra "My auntie says that outer space is where the aliens live!"

The entire class, including Miss Erinma all giggle.

"Now Kierra" Miss Erinma cautions. "While there are signs of intelligent life in space, we will not be discussing aliens in today's lesson. Today I would like to focus on the stars."

"What's a star?" Elijah asks.

"I'm glad you asked, Elijah! A star is a giant sphere of superhot gas. It's one of the big bright twinkles you see when you look in the sky at night before you go to bed."

"What makes a star so hot?" Edward asks.

"Good question Edward! Stars get hot by joining the element hydrogen into helium in a process called nuclear fusion. The nuclear fusion results in a huge amount of heat and light that looks like fire to us." says Miss Erinma.

"What is an element?" Adanna asks

GOLD

HYDROGEN

"I'm happy you ask! An element is a pure substance found on earth. Like hydrogen that is in the water we drink. Or the shiny sparkly gold we wear as jewelry," Miss Erinma explains.

ADANNA

Adanna ponders this word. Elements. And thinks about the stars she saw from her bedroom window the night before. Some twinkles were big, some small, and some were much brighter than others. She didn't realize that each twinkle was actually a large chemical reaction taking place right before her eyes. She smiles to herself as she thinks about the power of outer space.

"Why are some twinkles big, and other twinkles small?" Medina asks.

"At times the distance can make stars in the sky appear bigger or smaller. The biggest and brightest star of them all is the Sun. We see the sun everyday when we wake up and it gives us the light we need to live our lives." Miss Erinma explains.

"The sun is a star too?" Elijah asks

"That is right Elijah! Our sun is a star and you know how hot and fiery it is. The sun is the biggest star we can see because it is much closer to us than all the other stars in the galaxy. Collections of stars are called galaxies. Galaxies are made up of stars, dust and gas."

"I know what that is!" Medina blurts out "I went on a camping trip and saw the Big Dipper in the night sky."

"How nice Medina! Would you go on and describe to the class exactly what you saw."

"At night we were sitting around the campfire I looked into the sky and saw seven bright twinkles that looked like a cup. My camp counselor said it was the Big Dipper." Medina says

"That's correct Medina! The big dipper IS a group of stars but it is not considered a galaxy. The big dipper is called a **constellation.**

Scientists called Astronomers study these patterns in the sky." Miss Erinma replies, "A galaxy is made up of billions of stars!"

"What else is there in outer space?" Kierra asks.

"Astronomers have found lots of things in outer space! All types of other planets, galaxies, **vegetation** and other things are up there. We learned about the sun, so how about now we discuss the moon?" Miss Erinma suggests, holding up a picture of the moon

"The moon is very old. It was formed between 30 and 50 million years after our own planet Earth. Many, many years ago a large object hit our planet and blasted rocks off. The blast made the rocks melt together and when they cooled off they formed the moon that we see at night. Cool, right?"

"Cool!" the class echoed.

"Now we are almost finished with today's lesson. But I saved the best for last. I want to give you guys one last gem before you leave for the day. Have any of you guys heard of a shooting star?"

The class falls silent

"A shooting star is a small piece of rock that floats towards earth's **atmosphere**. It moves so fast that it heats up and glows as it comes towards earth. It can be seen at night because it is very bright and moves very, very fast."

"Wow!" Adanna exclaims. She has never heard of a moving twinkle. She is amazed by the thought of this.

"All right now pupils, that is all the outer space talk we have time for today. I do have a little homework assignment for you all. Tonight I want you all to look outside your bedroom window and take a long look at the night sky. Write down one interesting thing you notice. We will be sharing our findings in class tomorrow!"

STARS

FUSION   GALAXY

CONSTELLATION

VEGETATION

ATMOSPHERE

As Adanna gets into the car to go home, she thinks about all the cool new things she learned about outer space. She can't wait to go home and share the wonders of outer space with her mama.

"How was your first day, honey?" asks her mom.

"It was awesome, Mama! Today we learned about outer space, and stars and galaxies!"

"Wow sweetheart that is awesome! I'm glad to see you are enjoying your new school."

When it is dark, Adanna rushes to her bedroom window right before bed. She is excited to see what the night sky had in store for her.

She looks outside her night window into a dark void -- nothing is in the sky but the moon. And she knows that the plain old moon will not be fun news to share with her classmates.

She waits a few minutes more but sees nothing but a few twinkles here and there.

Adanna searches the sky high and low for anything she can see.

Just as she is about to give up, something catches the corner of her eye. It was the biggest and brightest twinkle she had ever seen, and it was moving fast!

"A shooting star!" she yells.

The shooting star zipped across the sky. It is bright red and fast. The way it soars across the sky is so beautiful.

Truly an amazing sight.

THE END

Vocabulary List

Atmosphere – The air surrounding earth.

Constellation – A group of stars.

Fusion – Joining two or more things together.

Galaxy – System of stars with gas or dust.

Vegetation – Plants in a habitat.

Vow – A promise.

Engagement Activities

1) Parents should review the vocabulary list with their child.

2) Parents should also bring their child outside to gaze at the stars.